Table of Contents

Essential Question

How do we respond to nature?

Notes

A Bird's Free Lunch

an excerpt from
The Wit of a Duck and Other Papers

by John Burroughs

John Burroughs (1837–1921) was a popular nature writer whose essays helped start the conservation movement. He was best known for his essays about birds, flowers, and rural scenes observed from his home in the Catskill Mountains of New York. Of his beloved home, Burroughs said, "Those hills comfort me as no other place in the world."

1   One winter, I fastened pieces of suet and marrow bones upon the tree in front of my window. Then, I sat at my desk and watched the birds eat their free lunch. The jays bossed the woodpeckers. The woodpeckers bossed the chickadees. And the chickadees bossed the kinglet.

2   The kinglet was the least of all, a sort of hop-o'-my-thumb[1] bird. He became quite tame, and one day alighted upon my arm as I stood leaning against the tree. I could have put my hand upon him several times. I wonder where he roosted. He was all alone. He liked the fare so well that he seemed disposed to stop till spring. During one terrible night of wind and snow and zero temperature I feared he would be swept away. I thought of him in the middle of the night, when the violence of the storm kept me from sleep.

1 hop-o'-my-thumb—very small; the reference is to the folktale character Tom Thumb, who could fit into the palm of a person's hand

3 Imagine this solitary atom in feathers drifting about in the great arctic out of doors and managing to survive. I fancied him in one of my thick spruces, his head under his tiny wing, buffeted by wind and snow, his little black feet clinging to the perch, and wishing that morning would come.

4 The fat meat is fuel for him. It keeps up the supply of animal heat. None of the birds will eat lean meat. They want the clear fat. The jays alight upon it and peck away with great vigor, almost standing on tiptoe to get the proper sweep. The woodpecker uses his head alone in pecking, but the jay's action involves the whole body. Yet his blows are softer, not so sharp and abrupt as those of the woodpecker. Pecking is not exactly his business.

red-headed woodpecker

blue jay

5

The Shimerdas

an excerpt from *My Ántonia*

by Willa Cather

Notes

My Ántonia (1918) is the third book in a trilogy[1] set in the prairie of the Great Plains in the late 1800s. The following excerpt, from chapter 2 in My Ántonia, *is narrated by the book's main character, Jim Burden, who is looking back on his past. In the beginning of the book, young Jim's parents have died. He travels by train from Virginia to his grandparents' farm in Nebraska. At the time, Nebraska was a new state, populated by hardy pioneers, many of them immigrants. One of those immigrants was Jim's friend and neighbor, a young Bohemian girl named Ántonia Shimerdas. Willa Cather (1873–1947) was a Pulitzer Prize–winning novelist. She created vividly drawn people and made the setting of the midwestern prairie come to life, as if it, too, were a character.*

1   While grandmother took the pitchfork we found standing in one of the rows and dug potatoes, while I picked them up out of the soft brown earth and put them into the bag, I kept looking up at the hawks that were doing what I might so easily do.

1 trilogy—a series of three creative works on one theme

◀ Willa Cather

2   When grandmother was ready to go, I said I would like to stay up there in the garden awhile.

3   She peered down at me from under her sunbonnet. "Aren't you afraid of snakes?"

4   "A little," I admitted, "but I like to stay, anyhow."

5   "Well, if you see one, don't have anything to do with him. The big yellow and brown ones won't hurt you; they're bull-snakes and help to keep the gophers down. Don't be scared if you see anything look out of that hole in the bank over there. That's a badger hole. He's about as big as a big 'possum, and his face is striped, black and white. He takes a chicken once in a while, but I won't let the men harm him. In a new country[2] a body feels friendly to the animals. I like to have him come out and watch me when I'm at work."

2 a new country—the reference is to Nebraska still being part wilderness and only recently being settled by pioneers

6   Grandmother swung the bag of potatoes over her shoulder and went down the path, leaning forward a little.

7   The road followed the windings of the draw;[3] when she came to the first bend, she waved at me and disappeared. I was left alone with this new feeling of lightness and content.

8   I sat down in the middle of the garden, where snakes could scarcely approach unseen, and leaned my back against a warm yellow pumpkin. There were some ground-cherry bushes growing along the furrows, full of fruit. I turned back the papery triangular sheaths that protected the berries and ate a few.

3 draw—a shallow gully

9 All about me giant grasshoppers, twice as big as any I had ever seen, were doing acrobatic feats among the dried vines. The gophers scurried up and down the ploughed ground. There in the sheltered draw bottom the wind did not blow very hard, but I could hear it singing its humming tune up on the level, and I could see the tall grasses wave. The earth was warm under me, and warm as I crumbled it through my fingers.

10 Odd little red bugs came out and moved in slow squadrons around me. Their backs were polished vermillion,[4] with black spots. I kept as still as I could. Nothing happened. I did not expect anything to happen. I was something that lay under the sun and felt it, like the pumpkins, and I did not want to be anything more. I was entirely happy.

11 Perhaps we feel like that when we die and become a part of something entire, whether it is sun and air, or goodness and knowledge. At any rate, that is happiness; to be dissolved into something complete and great. When it comes to one, it comes as naturally as sleep.

4 vermillion—a bright, red-orange color

The Birdseed Thief

1   Jason and his mother were true nature lovers. They loved all living things, especially birds. So it wasn't surprising when they decided to buy a bird feeder for their backyard.

2   The feeder they bought was mounted on a pole and designed to look like a little house. They chose what they thought was a good location, placing it near a big, leafy tree. Jason filled the feeder with a variety of food, including sunflower seeds and suet. Before long, the local birds were stopping by. Jason and Mom were delighted!

3   A week later, however, they saw that an unwelcome guest was helping itself to their bird food. A squirrel had jumped from the big tree to the feeder. It gobbled up the bird food!

4   Jason and Mom immediately moved the feeder away from the tree. However, that didn't deter the persistent creature. The next time, the squirrel brazenly climbed the pole and had itself a feast. The situation called for drastic measures! So Jason and Mom placed chicken wire around the feeder to prevent the squirrel from eating the food. Finally, the problem was solved!

5   The following day, Jason and Mom were in the backyard, watching the birds gather at the feeder. Then they noticed the squirrel searching the ground for food. Without saying a word, they went into the kitchen, filled a plastic bowl with nuts, and placed it by the big tree. They did exactly what true nature lovers would do!

BuildReflectWrite

Build Knowledge

How would you compare and contrast the descriptions of plants and animals in "A Bird's Free Lunch" (nonfiction) and "The Shimerdas" (fiction)? Record your ideas and then write a short summary of important similarities and differences.

	"A Bird's Free Lunch"	"The Shimerdas"
Similarities		
Differences		
Summary:		

Reflect

How do we respond to nature?

Based on this week's texts, write down new ideas and questions you have about the essential question.

_____

_____

_____

_____

_____

_____

_____

Building Research Skills

Narrative

Pretend you are going to write a narrative story about someone who observes nature in New York's Catskill Mountains. One of your guiding research questions is: What plants and animals are commonly seen in the Catskills? Read and take notes from two or more sources to find facts and details to help you answer this question. List the sources of your information.

Remember to annotate as you read.

Notes

Being in and Seeing Nature:

The Writing of John Burroughs

by Jeffrey Fuerst

1   Pioneering nature writer John Burroughs (1837–1921) found his artistic voice and also a sense of delight and wonder by carefully observing the world around him. He grew up on a farm in Delaware County, New York. As a boy, one of his favorite things to do after completing his chores was to escape to a special place he later called "Boyhood Rock." Burroughs liked to look out from this spot on Old Clump Mountain, a part of the Catskills, and think deeply about what he was seeing.

2   Burroughs's habit of studying and reflecting on nature stayed with him his entire life. He became a teacher and government worker, and also gained fame writing essays for magazines. By the 1880s, Burroughs had become a full-time writer. He wrote of fishing and hiking. He wrote about the seasons. He wrote about the birds, flowers, and animals he saw outside his window.

3   Burroughs spent most of his life near where he grew up. In summers, he preferred the view from a small cabin in the woods. He named this place "Slabsides"—and from it he recorded the daily lives and interactions of his animal neighbors.

Observing the Natural World

In the poem "Waiting" below, Burroughs marvels at the timelessness of nature. The natural world goes about its business without care or concern for man-made time. Burroughs accepts that life, like nature, cannot be controlled.

Waiting

Serene, I fold my hands and wait,
Nor care for wind, nor tide, nor sea;
I rave no more 'gainst time or fate,
For lo! my own shall come to me.

5 I stay my haste, I make delays,
For what avails this eager pace?
I stand amid the eternal ways,
And what is mine shall know my face.

Asleep, awake, by night or day,
10 The friends I seek are seeking me;
No wind can drive my bark astray,
Nor change the tide of destiny.

What matter if I stand alone?
I wait with joy the coming years;
15 My heart shall reap where it hath sown,
And garner up its fruit of tears.

The waters know their own and draw
The brook that springs in yonder height;
So flows the good with equal law
20 Unto the soul of pure delight.

The stars come nightly to the sky;
The tidal wave unto the sea;
Nor time, nor space, nor deep, nor high,
Can keep my own away from me.

"Slabsides,"
Burroughs's cabin in
Roxbury, New York

4   Burroughs is often praised for his descriptive writing. Its style of observation is more literary than scientific. He takes the reader on the same personal journey he is experiencing, narrating the events.

5   His gentle, lyrical writing gives a human dimension to nonhuman subjects. For example, in "The Chipmunk,"* Burroughs observes the main character emerging from its winter nest. Now rested, the chipmunk is ready for a glorious spring.

The Chipmunk (excerpts)

6   *The first chipmunk in March is as sure a token of the spring as the first bluebird or the first robin. And it is quite as welcome. Some genial influence has found him out there in his burrow, deep under the ground. And waked him up and enticed him forth into the light of day. The red squirrel has been more or less active all winter. His track has dotted the surface of every new-fallen snow throughout the season. But the chipmunk retired from view early in December. He has passed the rigorous months in his nest. He rests beside his hoard of nuts, some feet underground. When he emerges in March and is seen upon his little journeys along the fences—or perched upon a log or rock near his hole in the woods—it is another sign that spring is at hand.*

*from *Squirrels and Other Fur-Bearers* (1901)

7   Burroughs's essays often have a poetic quality. In the next two passages from "The Chipmunk," Burroughs uses personification when he gives human characteristics to the chipmunk. He also compares the animal's actions to those of human beings. The chipmunk becomes much like a character in a story.

8   *The chipmunk is quite a solitary creature. I have never known more than one to occupy the same den. Apparently no two can agree to live together. What a clean, pert, dapper, nervous little fellow he is!*

9   *How fast his heart beats, as he stands up on the wall by the roadside. With his hands spread out upon his breast, he regards you intently! A movement of your arm, and he darts into the wall with a saucy chip-r-r sound. It has the effect of slamming the door behind him.*

10 Burroughs now develops his main character, the chipmunk, by describing its actions. Note, though, that Burroughs—as the storyteller—is part of the story, too.

11 *I was much amused one October in watching a chipmunk carry nuts and other food into his den.*

12 *He had made a well-defined path from his door out through the weeds and dry leaves into the territory where his feeding ground lay. The path was a crooked one. It dipped under weeds, under some large, loosely piled stones, under a pile of chestnut posts—then followed the remains of an old wall.*

13   *Going and coming, his motions were like clockwork.*

14   *He would pause a breath with one foot raised, slip quickly a few yards over some dry leaves, pause again by a stump beside a path, rush across the path to the pile of loose stones, go under the first and over the second, gain the pile of posts, make his way through that, survey his course a half moment from the other side of it, and then dart on to some other cover, and presently beyond my range, where I think he gathered acorns, as there were no other nut-bearing trees than oaks near.*

15   *In four or five minutes I would see him coming back, always keeping rigidly to the course he took going out, pausing at the same spots, darting over or under the same objects, clearing at a bound the same pile of leaves. There was no variation in his manner of proceeding all the time I observed him.*

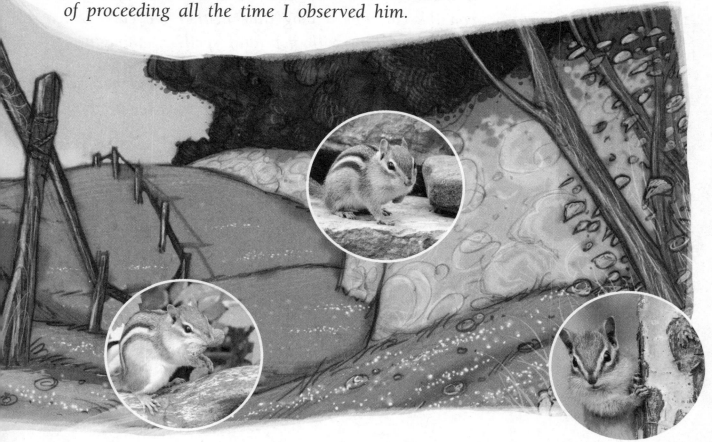

16   A good storyteller must do more than create appealing characters. Burroughs fills his writing with drama. It is the natural excitement found in the wild. In the next passage, Burroughs sees a cat also observing the chipmunk. He describes the actions of the predator and the prey. He further engages the reader by wondering what the cat and the chipmunk will do.

17   *One summer day I watched a cat for nearly a half hour trying her arts upon a chipmunk that sat upon a pile of stone. Evidently her game was to stalk him. She had cleared half the distance, or about twelve feet, that separated the chipmunk from a dense Norway spruce, when I chanced to become a spectator of the little drama. There sat the cat crouched low on the grass, her big, yellow eyes fixed upon the chipmunk, and there sat the chipmunk at the mouth of his den, motionless, with his eyes fixed upon the cat. For a long time neither moved. "Will the cat bind him with her fatal spell?" I thought.*

18   *Sometimes her head slowly lowered and her eyes seemed to dilate, and I fancied she was about to spring. But she did not.*

19   *The chipmunk finally quickly entered his den. The cat soon slunk away.*

John Burroughs fishing in Yellowstone National Park, in 1906

20   Burroughs was a lifelong nature writer who kept his eyes, ears, and heart open. He observed the world around him. He brought out its energy in a personal way, giving it a deeper, emotional meaning. It is as if the reader is experiencing Burroughs's experience at the same time, making his view of the natural world ours, too. Toward the end of his life, Burroughs wrote in "The Summit of the Years" about the time he had spent observing nature:

21   *The longer I live the more my mind dwells upon the beauty and wonder of the world. . . . I have loved the feel of the grass under my feet, and the sound of the running streams by my side. The hum of the wind in the tree tops has always been good music to me, and the face of the fields has often comforted me more than the faces of men. I am in love with this world.*

Waiting for Spring

1   Chipmunks and robins are not the only signs of spring. Each year on February 2, crowds of people eagerly gather in Punxsutawney, Pennsylvania, to watch the famous groundhog known as Punxsutawney Phil. They are there to observe this furry creature emerge from its burrow and predict when spring will arrive. Will spring be early or late? According to tradition, if it is sunny and Phil sees its shadow, there will be six more weeks of winter weather. If it is cloudy and Phil doesn't see its shadow, spring will come early. The Groundhog Day officials make it look as if Phil is whispering in their ear.

2   The Groundhog Day tradition began more than a thousand years ago in Europe. Back then, people believed animals that hibernate could predict when spring would come. They thought that if a bear woke up and saw its shadow, there would be several more weeks of winter. If the bear didn't see its shadow, spring would arrive early. When these people came to America, some of them settled in Pennsylvania. They continued the custom—but used the groundhog, instead of the bear. In 1886, February 2 was proclaimed Groundhog Day.

3   Some states have adopted their own groundhogs. However, Punxsutawney Phil is still the most famous one. Although this furry forecaster is often wrong, it doesn't seem to matter much. That's probably because people have such a good time on Groundhog Day!

BuildReflectWrite

Build Knowledge

Write down examples of nature imagery from each of the John Burroughs texts. Based on your choices, what conclusion would you draw about some of the key differences between images used in poetry and images used in nonfiction? Are there similarities, too?

"Waiting" Images	"The Chipmunk" Images
Examples 1. 2. 3.	**Examples** 1. 2. 3.
Conclusion:	

Reflect

How do we respond to nature?

Based on this week's texts, write down new ideas and questions you have about the essential question.

_____

_____

_____

_____

_____

_____

Building Research Skills

Informative/Explanatory

Imagine that you have been asked to write an informative essay about how different animals survive the winter. One of your guiding questions is: How do chipmunks live during the winter? Read and take notes from two or more approved sources to answer this question.

Remember to annotate as you read.

Notes

Birches

by Robert Frost

When I see birches bend to left and right
Across the lines of straighter darker trees,
I like to think some boy's been swinging them.
But swinging doesn't bend them down to stay
5 As ice-storms do. Often you must have seen them
Loaded with ice a sunny winter morning
After a rain. They click upon themselves
As the breeze rises, and turn many-colored
As the stir cracks and crazes their enamel.
10 Soon the sun's warmth makes them shed crystal shells
Shattering and avalanching on the snow-crust—
Such heaps of broken glass to sweep away
You'd think the inner dome of heaven had fallen.
They are dragged to the withered bracken[1] by the load,
15 And they seem not to break; though once they are bowed
So low for long, they never right themselves:
You may see their trunks arching in the woods
Years afterwards, trailing their leaves on the ground
Like girls on hands and knees that throw their hair
20 Before them over their heads to dry in the sun.

1 bracken—a fern-like plant, or a cluster of these plants

birches on
a winter
morning

Robert Frost (1874–1963) was a popular poet, highly regarded for his realistic portrayals of nature and the rural life. His descriptions of New England settings, landscapes, and wildlife get the reader to think about deeper social issues and philosophical themes.

Notes

But I was going to say when Truth broke in
With all her matter-of-fact about the ice-storm
I should prefer to have some boy bend them
As he went out and in to fetch the cows—
25 Some boy too far from town to learn baseball,
Whose only play was what he found himself,
Summer or winter, and could play alone.
One by one he subdued[2] his father's trees
By riding them down over and over again
30 Until he took the stiffness out of them,
And not one but hung limp, not one was left
For him to conquer. He learned all there was
To learn about not launching out too soon
And so not carrying the tree away
35 Clear to the ground. He always kept his poise[3]
To the top branches, climbing carefully
With the same pains you use to fill a cup
Up to the brim, and even above the brim.

2 subdued—conquered
3 poise—balance; bearing

birches in
summer

Then he flung outward, feet first, with a swish,
40 Kicking his way down through the air
   to the ground.
So was I once myself a swinger of birches.
And so I dream of going back to be.
It's when I'm weary of considerations,
And life is too much like a pathless wood
45 Where your face burns and tickles
   with the cobwebs
Broken across it, and one eye is weeping
From a twig's having lashed across it open.
I'd like to get away from earth awhile
And then come back to it and begin over.
50 May no fate willfully misunderstand me
And half grant what I wish and snatch me away
Not to return. Earth's the right place for love:
I don't know where it's likely to go better.
I'd like to go by climbing a birch tree,
55 And climb black branches up a snow-white trunk
Toward heaven, till the tree could bear no more,
But dipped its top and set me down again.
That would be good both going and coming
   back.
One could do worse than be a swinger
   of birches.

birches in
fall

In Summer

by Paul Laurence Dunbar

Oh, summer has clothed the earth
In a cloak from the loom of the sun!
And a mantle,[1] too, of the skies' soft blue,
And a belt where the rivers run.

5   And now for the kiss of the wind,
And the touch of the air's soft hands,
With the rest from strife and the heat of life,
With the freedom of lakes and lands.

I envy the farmer's boy
10   Who sings as he follows the plow;
While the shining green of the young blades lean
To the breezes that cool his brow.

He sings to the dewy morn,
No thought of another's ear;
15   But the song he sings is a chant for kings
And the whole wide world to hear.

1 mantle—something that covers

Paul Laurence Dunbar (1872–1906) was a poet, novelist, and playwright, and one of the first African American writers to gain a national following. His poetry has continued to inspire contemporary poets.

Notes

He sings of the joys of life,
Of the pleasures of work and rest,
From an o'erfull heart, without aim or art;
20 'T is a song of the merriest.

O ye who toil[2] in the town,
And ye who moil[3] in the mart,
Hear the artless song, and your faith made strong
Shall renew your joy of heart.

25 Oh, poor were the worth of the world
If never a song were heard,—
If the sting of grief had no relief,
And never a heart were stirred.

So, long as the streams run down,
30 And as long as the robins trill,
Let us taunt old Care with a merry air,
And sing in the face of ill.

2 toil—to work hard and long
3 moil—to work hard, usually at a lowly, physically difficult job

Word Study Read

Remember to annotate as you read.

Notes

Birch Bark Canoes

1   Birch trees have always grown in the forests of the Northeast. When Native Americans lived in the area long ago, they recognized and valued this gift from nature. They figured out that the outer bark of white birches could be used to make useful things, such as wigwam coverings and food containers. However, the most important item they created was the birch bark canoe.

2   The birch bark canoe was lightweight but sturdy. It could carry heavy loads for long distances. The Native Americans made the canoe in different sizes depending on its use. A small hunting canoe was eight to ten feet long. It could carry two people. A large canoe used for transporting goods was twenty-four feet long. It could carry up to ten people.

3   Building a birch bark canoe took several weeks. First, the birch bark was peeled from the tree and laid on the ground. Then it was covered with heavy stones to make it flat. Next, it was placed on a frame made of poles and stakes. This formed the shape of the canoe. The ends of the birch bark were then pulled together and tied with root fibers. To make the canoe waterproof, the seams were glued with pine gum and charcoal.

4   When European explorers sailed to the northeastern coast of America in the 1500s, they were amazed by these graceful canoes that moved swiftly in water. In fact, these traditional canoes were so well designed that they became the models for today's canoes made of aluminum and fiberglass.

BuildReflectWrite

Build Knowledge

Write down your responses to the two poems you read this week. Then think about why each poet decided to write a poem about nature. Jot down your ideas about the author's purpose.

	Ideas About the Poem	Ideas About the Author's Purpose
"Birches"		
"In Summer"		

Reflect

How do we respond to nature?

Based on this week's texts, write down new ideas and questions you have about the essential question.

_____

_____

_____

_____

_____

Building Research Skills

Opinion

Would you prefer to observe nature in New England or the Mojave Desert? To develop an opinion, conduct research using this guiding question: What are the natural features of these two regions? Read and take notes from two or more sources to answer the question. List your sources.

Support for Collaborative Conversation

Discussion Prompts

Express ideas or opinions . . .

When I read _____, it made me think that _____.

Based on the information in _____, my [opinion/idea] is _____.

As I [listened to/read/watched] _____, it occurred to me that _____.

It was important that _____.

Gain the floor . . .

I would like to add a comment. _____.

Excuse me for interrupting, but _____.

That made me think of _____.

Build on a peer's idea or opinion . . .

That's an interesting point. It makes me think _____.

If _____, then maybe _____.

[Name] said _____. That could mean that _____.

Express agreement with a peer's idea . . .

I agree that _____ because _____.

I also feel that _____ because _____.

[Name] made the comment that _____, and I think that is important because _____.

Respectfully express disagreement . . .

I understand your point of view that _____, but in my opinion _____ because _____.

That is an interesting idea, but did you consider the fact that _____?

I do not agree that _____. I think that _____ because _____.

Ask a clarifying question . . .

You said _____. Could you explain what you mean by that?

I don't understand how your evidence supports that inference. Can you say more?

I'm not sure I understand. Are you saying that _____?

Clarify for others . . .

When I said _____, what I meant was that _____.

I reached my conclusion because _____.

Group Roles

Discussion Director:
Your role is to guide the group's discussion and be sure that everyone has a chance to express his or her ideas.

Notetaker:
Your job is to record the group's ideas and important points of discussion.

Summarizer:
In this role, you will restate the group's comments and conclusions.

Presenter:
Your role is to provide an overview of the group's discussion to the class.

Timekeeper:
You will track the time and help to keep your peers on task.